Unlock the
Miracle
Within

Copyright © 2023 Ursula D. Knecht

All rights reserved. No part of this publication may be reproduced, distributed, or transmitted in any form or by any means, including photocopying, recording, or other electronic or mechanical methods, without the prior written permission of the publisher, except in the case of brief quotations embodied in critical reviews and certain other noncommercial uses permitted by copyright law.

(✽) **green**hill

https://greenhillpublishing.com.au/

Knecht, Ursula D. (author)
Unlock the Miracle Within
ISBN 978-1-923088-77-1 (paperback)
ISBN 978-1-923156-23-4 (hardcover)
Self Help

Typeset Calluna 11/18
Cover Image by Adobe Stock
Book design by Green Hill

Unlock the Miracle Within

URSULA D. KNECHT

"This book goes a step further than other self-help books. It provides links to hypnosis sessions that are designed to more deeply embed the learning within you. The 5 Steps are explained clearly, and there is not too much to take in at each stage. Ursula Knecht is there to gently support you through the process, guiding with kindness and humility. Making change is not easy, but with the hypnosis, working through the 5 Steps is simple and pleasant."

LISA LARK

DEEPLY GRATEFUL TO:

Marianne for her support and encouragement over the last 26 years of my life's journey.

And to all my friends and family supporting me over the years.

Contents

How this book works	1
5 Steps to Unlock The Miracle Within	4
Before you start	5
Introduction	6
What blocks to success are limiting your life?	8
These are the 5 Steps:	8
Step One: The Miracle Question	11
Open your mind to new possibilities	11
Open yourself up to new possibilities	19
Recommendation	22
Ask the Miracle Question	23
Visualise	23
Pretend the Miracle Has Happened	24
Expressive Writing: A Secret Tool	27
Focus on uplifting thoughts and your positive future vision	29
Here are some more suggestions:	30
Checklist	31

Step Two: The indisputable truth about you	**33**
Emotions can shape snowflakes and water	34
How to deceive your subconscious mind into positivity	40
Human emotion can even be measured	41
Imagine your new world	42
Another way to picture human emotions	44
How Dr David Hawkins measured emotions	44
How to love yourself: a step-by-step guide	47
Here are some steps you can take	
to cultivate self-love:	47
Summary	50
Hypnosis Session Review	51
Step 3: Let go of your past and be free to live as you	**53**
Empower the positive feelings in your mind and body	60
Listen to your inner voices – feel your emotions	61
How can you evolve through	
changing shape? Literally!	62
Never judge a book by its cover	64
Turn away from darkness and look into light and hope	65
What do you say to yourself?	66
What would it take to find better answers every day?	71
A process to free yourself from limiting beliefs	74
Make peace with your past	76
Summary	81
Checklist	84

Step 4: Discover your hidden potential   **87**

   How to visualise your future   90

   Another Crucial Key to Achieving Your Goals   99

      Asking better questions opens your
        world to new possibilities   99

   Choose your thoughts wisely –
    they can be life-changing   103

   Checklist   105

Step 5: Live your life on your terms   **107**

   Define Your Values   109

   Guide to defining your values   110

   Life Balance   112

      The 80/20 Rule   116

      Here is the theory of the Pareto Principle: 117

   Goal Setting   119

   Setting meaningful life goals   120

   Checklist   124

Final Thoughts   **127**

References   **130**

How this book works

This workbook is a step-by-step guide to reprogramming your mind to become the best version of yourself. I devised the 5-Step process so I could share the secrets of my hypnosis experience. My clients already benefit significantly from working through these 5 Steps. The experience has been highly successful and life-changing for them.

As you work through the book, you will be directed to my webpage, where you will find audio, visualisation, hypnosis and meditation sessions designed to work alongside each step. These sessions form a powerful part of the process that will lead you through the five easy steps of conscious and subconscious changes.

You may already be familiar with meditation, which involves focusing or clearing your mind to relax and reduce anxiety and stress. I regularly use hypnosis in my clinical practice, as a pleasant and powerful way to achieve lasting change. Hypnosis is a safe way to overcome your limiting thoughts and the beliefs that are deeply engraved in your mind. The subconscious mind seems to know about your full potential and your thoughts about yourself. None of my clients' subconscious minds have ever rejected the truth about themselves. The more you are aware of this truth, the easier the exercises will be.

As you work through the 5 Steps, you will automatically develop more extraordinary visions for your future and you will see yourself more and more through loving and caring eyes. You can revisit the hypnosis sessions as often as you wish, and I recommend that you do this in order to gain more and more benefit from them. Please especially take whatever time you need to harvest the benefits from the Step 2 hypnosis session, and then move on and read the chapter.

Now you can unlock your full potential. If you are ready for change, the unique combination of hypnosis with this workbook will make the 5-Step process a pleasant, life-changing experience.

Should you have any problems along the way, please do not hesitate to contact me at:

ursula@hypnosis-joondalup.com.au.

Now, let's get started. I look forward to learning how this book and the audio help you on your life journey.

To an inspired life

Ursula Knecht
Clinical Hypnotherapist
0468 858 466
ursula@hypnosis-joondalup.com.au
https://hypnosis-joondalup.com.au

5 Steps to Unlock The Miracle Within

STEP 1: The Miracle Question	*Online Session*: The Miracle Question Meditation
STEP 2: Improve Your Self-Image	*Online Session*: Hypnosis to Internalise the Truth About Yourself
STEP 3: Let Go Of Your Past And Be Free To Live As You	*Online Sessions*: 1. Hypnosis for Letting Go and Healing Your Past 2. Hypnosis to Make Peace with Your Past – Forgiveness
STEP 4: Unlock Your Hidden Potential	*Online Session*: The Hidden Garden Hypnosis
STEP 5: Live Your Life On Your Terms	*Online Session*: Hypnosis for Future Vision and Goal Setting

Please share your journey and ask questions in the private Facebook group.
https://hypnosis-joondalup.com.au/Unlock-the-Miracle-Within

Before you start

You will need access to the accompanying online sessions as you work through the 5 Steps in this workbook.

Before you start, go online and sign up to follow the audio, visualisation and hypnosis sessions as you work through the 5 Steps.

sign up
https://hypnosis-joondalup.com.au/miracle

login for book readers
https://hypnosis-joondalup.com.au/miracle-login/

Introduction

Do you know deep inside that you could be more? What life could you be living if you unlocked your full potential?

The 5 Steps in this book aim to guide you to discover your inner self and have the courage to fully live your life. What if it could set you free so you can live a prosperous and happy life?

I am writing this book to help you live a fulfilled and happy life. Alongside the book, I will guide you through safe and relaxing hypnosis sessions so that you become aware of any unhelpful subconscious programs that hinder you from becoming the person you seek to be. The subconscious mind is the higher and more powerful part of the mind.

This easy 5-step process will guide you step by step through a process that aims to reveal the real you. Who could you become if you were free of all limiting programming and beliefs about your past?

I have been reading self-help books since my teenage years: *Awaken the Giant Within* (Anthony Robbins), *Think and Grow Rich* (Napoleon Hill), and *The Secret* (Rhonda Byrne), to name a few. As a hypnotherapist, I have wondered if something is missing from these books. Why do they work so well for some people but not others? And why are "successful" people often unsuccessful in almost every of their life?

I share personal stories in these pages to illustrate life's ups and downs. I hope they motivate you to move forward and explore your hidden gifts and talents. I am opening my heart to you, trusting that you will read these stories with a kind and open heart. My deepest desire is that this book, with my stories, will touch and inspire you to become that unique person you are meant to be.

What blocks to success are limiting your life?

Clients usually seek help from a hypnotherapist when all other avenues have failed, so the clients I see are desperate for change. I have been honoured to guide them through the straightforward and life-changing 5-Step program, helping them to make profound changes along the way.

If you are ready for change and want to improve your life, this book is for you. If you have a clear goal for the outcome of this program, I challenge you to keep an open mind. You might discover and unlock much more than you could ever have imagined, and open your mind to new life-changing opportunities.

These are the 5 Steps:
1. The Miracle Question - open your mind to new possibilities.
2. Improve your self-image – discover the indisputable truth about yourself.
3. Become aware of limiting beliefs, set yourself free from inner limitations, and heal from your past.
4. Unlock your hidden potential in the Hidden Garden hypnosis session.
5. Recreate your life - visualise your ideal future.

This is not just a simple workbook. The combination with online hypnosis sessions makes it a unique, pleasant and powerful journey of self-discovery. As you work through the book, at each stage you will find the links to the relevant online hypnosis sessions designed to streamline your transformation. The powerful hypnosis sessions aim to change your subconscious programs so you can set yourself free for a fantastic future.

If you have never experienced hypnosis, you may not know how relaxing and peaceful it is. What do my clients say?

"I just come to you to sleep, and positive changes are happening."

"This is such a peaceful and blissful state, I did not want to return."

"I never thought this would work, but now I can..."

Hypnosis has been around for centuries, so its success is not questioned. The question is whether you will let it work for you.

If you are ready to see yourself and your life in a new light, start with Step 1. Open your subconscious to new possibilities and, step by step, experience life transformation. The stories I share show how you can visualise your goal, overcome hurdles, and eventually celebrate victory.

STEP ONE

The Miracle Question

_____

Open your mind to new possibilities

What defining moment leads you to read this here, right now? Are you at a crossroads? Not sure where you want to go, but you know you want to change your life? This is the ideal point to make critical changes that will enhance your life profoundly.

> *Remember, too, that all who succeed in life get off to a bad start and pass through many heartbreaking struggles before they "arrive." The turning point in the lives of those who succeed usually comes at the moment of some crisis, through which they are introduced to their other selves.* [1]

I will share some of my defining moments with you, hoping you will be inspired to bring to light your unique being. Here is my first story.

Why abandon a superbly running business? (Part 1)

Everything was going extraordinarily well – at least, it was for anyone looking at my life from the outside. In my mid-30s, I ran a very successful physio practice and gym; I was well-known in the area for my excellent service and skilled physiotherapy. To the observer, it looked like I had it all.

People did not see that I worked my butt off. In fact, I was working for 70 hours a week. I only took two weeks off every year, to keep the business running and cover my high fixed costs. I could not afford to be away longer and work less as I was not only under financial pressure, I was afraid of losing clients and disappointing those who made referrals. Running on this hamster wheel, I had no time for self-reflection; I just continued. I was young and fit, with no back pain anymore.

>  **You can read my chronic back pain story on my webpage:**
> physio-joondalup.com.au

Are you in a hamster wheel, constantly repeating each day, each week? When in a fixed pattern, you make sense of it and keep going in the same way without challenging it.

I was a success story from the outside, running a thriving clinic. My physiotherapy schedule was fully booked, and I had expanded my business with massage and a fully equipped gym. So, on the one hand, I was excited. On the other hand, I was exhausted.

Then, a transformational moment happened.

Entirely out of the blue and shortly before Christmas, Rose, a good friend, started to have some tummy aches. Nobody thought that something sinister was happening to her. Rose had to stay in the hospital, where I visited her over Christmas. How shocking to see a beautiful young person fading away from abdominal cancer. She had been a very compassionate and skilled nurse working in a hospital where I had once worked. I'm not sure if it was January or early February when Rose passed away. Why Rose?

Why? My inner world crumbled, and I had many questions and no answers. Rose was such a loving, kind, and compassionate person, beautiful inside and outside. She had a healthy lifestyle, so why? I could not understand this. It did not make any sense at all! I was devastated and deeply shocked. The world made no sense to me. Why would this happen to a person like her? What is life all about? I felt betrayed by life. There was no justice. Why had God taken her away so early? My heart was hurting. I was overcome by sadness and emptiness, and a massive vacuum opened in my chest.

What was life about? Running on a hamster wheel, and then? Rose was a similar age to me. Her sudden death stopped me in my tracks.

My unanswered questions led to big life changes for me.

Take a moment to reflect on your life.

As you read this, you might find that you are at a similar time in your life,

seeking answers to the most profound question:
What is your life purpose?

I took a step back and started reflecting on my life. What did I want in this life? What was my purpose? I loved travelling and exploring the world, but they were not possible with the demands of this business.

What was I passionate about? Was it worthwhile to keep my business and running in this hamster wheel?

While dwelling on my life questions, I began to observe people more closely. Why was there such a massive gap in the results of similar clients? Why did clients with the same problem, similar age, and profession have such different outcomes from my physio treatment?

While I was seeking answers, looking at life with an open mind and asking many questions, I found an exciting brochure in my letter box. This brochure was the start of a life-changing journey for me. Perhaps this book will be the same for you.

The brochure was about a forthcoming seminar on overcoming life's challenges. My partner, Marianne, and I were ready for change and attended it.

The seminar, presented by Martin Betschart, was all about life changes. It was held in a big hotel room with perhaps 200 attendees. Martin opened my mind to reflect on my own limiting beliefs and mindset. We were informed that by the end of the day, we would all walk over burning hot charcoal. In the afternoon, we could see them making the fire that would be ready at the end of the day.

The day was about what Bob Proctor called that "piece of real estate between our ears". The limiting thoughts and beliefs we grow up with, and what we accumulate over the years, define what we can or cannot do.

The symbolism of the fire walk was to leave the past behind, including fears, guilt, hurt and pain, and arrive at the other end ready to start life afresh, as an empty book for us to write in. This book aims to guide you to do precisely this, through the 5-Step process.

How does walking over burning charcoal make you feel when you think about it? At first, we were all afraid, but the longer the day went on, the more we learned about the mind and its capacity, the more excited we got.

The mental preparation was mind-blowing. I had never come across this kind of information before. I was utterly unaware of all the limiting beliefs I had deeply engraved in my being. The fire walk preparation went deep into the subconscious programs, limiting us from moving forward. Learning that there was much more in life than running on that hamster wheel felt so good! I was ready to open my mind to new possibilities. There was more to life than I had experienced so far.

By the end of the day, we had a clear list of what we were prepared to let go of, and we were open to new possibilities on the other side of the fire.

Alexas_Fotos [2]

The seminar with the fire walk was the start of a series of weekends with Marin Betschart. Much of his teaching was based on neurolinguistic programming. We were also trained in communication, public speaking, and goal setting.

The most life-shifting weekend, in a stunning 5-star hotel, was about life visioning. I remember that it was a warm, bright, sunny day when the following happened.

After the life visioning session, Marianne said, "I was jogging on the red soil in my dream vision!" I was stunned. "Really? That's strange," I said. "You have never been to Australia, so why would you be running on red soil?" She replied: "And along the ocean!"

Strange. Marianne and I had not spoken much about my travels to Australia in 1996. How would she come up with this future vision? Of course, when we arrived home after that weekend, I went to the cellar and got all the old photo books from my trip in 1996.

Walking over burning charcoal was a life-transforming moment for me. My deepest desire in writing this book is that you will experience the same invigorating life changes. By following the 5 Steps, you will be guided through the process towards becoming aware of your limiting beliefs and opening your mind to new possibilities.

Could this process open your mind to new possibilities you would never have thought of? What guidance might you receive? What pictures will you see when you open your mind to new opportunities?

Open yourself up to new possibilities

Since you are still reading, perhaps you have a feeling – or even a knowing – that you could become much more than you are today. Are you ready to explore that miracle and bring your hidden gifts and talents to light? Are you ready to live a more fulfilled, happier life?

Here is where your life-changing journey begins. This is the start to becoming your best self, finding your purpose, inner peace, and power. Imagine where you would be after walking over burning charcoal. Open your mind and visualise where you could be in 3-5 years.

Welcome to a pleasant journey where you will relax, your inner peace will grow, and fear and anxiety will dissolve more and more. Seeing people calm down, discovering their passion, and finding peace within themselves, is one of the most rewarding experiences I have had as a hypnotherapist.

Remember to be kind to yourself. If this is new to you, take it easy and be patient.

You might find it helpful to listen to the recording on my webpage a few times:
Https://Hypnosis-Joondalup.Com.Au/Miracle-Login/

Jplenio [2]

The first Step is to ask the Miracle Question, to open your mind to the miracle inside you that is waiting to be unlocked. The Miracle Question is a beautiful and potent way to start life changes. It is one of the key techniques in solution-focused therapy. [3]

> *Solution-Focused Brief Therapy (SFBT)*
> *is a short-term goal-focused evidence-based*
> *therapeutic approach, which incorporates*
> *positive psychology principles and practices,*
> *and which helps clients change by constructing*
> *solutions rather than focusing on problems.*

In the most basic sense, SFBT is a hope friendly, positive emotion eliciting, future-oriented vehicle for formulating, motivating, achieving, and sustaining desired behavioural change.

Asking the Miracle Question is just the beginning of working towards your final future vision. The journey involves discovering the unique, precious, talented, and gifted you. The further you travel on this journey, the easier it will be to see yourself in this positive light. Even if it is difficult to grasp initially, you are unique and you are here in this world for your specific purpose.

It is essential to be kind to yourself and let things happen as you work through the process and the hypnosis sessions. Please understand that I want the best for you.

It might feel strange if you have not yet experienced visualising relaxation. That is OK. Don't worry if you can't "see" anything. Your subconscious has many ways to communicate, including visualising, feeling, and through your senses of smell and taste. The more you do it, the easier it will become. Remember, as Tony Robbins taught, repetition is the mother of all skills.

Recommendation

Start and/or end your day with the following meditation.

The more you do so, the more you will feel at peace, and you will begin to see your future life of freedom to be yourself unfold in more colour and detail.

Go to the webpage and listen to it here:
https://hypnosis-joondalup.com.au/miracle-login/

Darkmoon_Art [2]

Let's get started!

Have a notebook ready so you can write down your impressions, thoughts and responses.

Ask the Miracle Question

Visualise

Find a quiet space where you can relax for about 10 to 15 minutes. (Use the recorded online session, or read this and then go through it in your mind).

- Close your eyes, take three deep breaths. Breathe in relaxation. Breathe out stress, worries and whatever hinders you from being present here and now.
- Imagine that you are falling into a deep, peaceful, relaxing sleep tonight.
- It is peaceful, restful sleep. You are so profoundly asleep that you don't notice anything around you.
- While you are asleep, a miracle happens.
- It might be an angel, a light… a magic, loving and healing touch.
- The miracle takes away all your worries, doubts, fears, guilt, hurt, pain and whatever else hinders you from being free and the true you.
- As you are so soundly asleep, you don't consciously know this miracle is happening.
- When you wake up in the morning, how will you notice that the miracle has happened?

- What will you think about yourself?
- How will you move?
- How will your body feel?
- What will you do?
- How will your day look?
- What will you say to yourself and others?
- Would your coffee or tea smell and taste differently?
- Does the day shine more brightly?
- Just sit there for a while and focus on your life from now on. How does it look, feel, taste, and smell?
- Now, take a moment and write about this imaginary life. How miraculous could your life be?

This is a magical way to start and end your day. Who knows what treasures you might find within?

Pretend the Miracle Has Happened

You have focused on these thoughts and feelings and imagined your ideal life. How would it be if you could make this vision a reality by pretending two or three times a day for about 20 to 30 minutes?

- Pretend that the miracle has happened. You have decided that this is your 20 minutes. You are motivated and keen to focus on your beautiful future vision, when all these negative thoughts rush into your mind!

If this is new to you, it can feel overwhelming when you suddenly become aware of your negative self-talk. What can you do? How do you stop this chatter and focus on your miracle vision? The most effective way to stop the chatter is to talk to your subconscious. Sounds strange? That is OK. Humour me and do it anyway; you will be surprised how well this works:

- Acknowledge the thoughts.
- Tell them that this is your time to focus on new thoughts about creating your better future. Say that you will listen to them again in 20 or 30 minutes, or whatever time frame you have set aside to live in your miracle world.

The more often you do this, the more you become aware of your negative self-talk, and the easier it is to deal with the subconscious chatter. Initially, this might feel strange or overwhelming. However, that is a good sign because before, it was the voice in your head that you constantly listened to unfiltered. It had always accessed your mind, never stopping even when you were not aware of it. The more you can turn it into an uplifting, positive voice, the more positive and inspirational your life will become.

If all this is new to you, consider spending one to three weeks on each step. Of course, you can keep reading and see what is next, gathering an overview of the next transformational step. However, to achieve profound and lasting change, finding the correct pace for yourself is vital so you can feel better every day, with more uplifting thoughts, and feeling happier from the inside out.

When you practise the Miracle Question visualisation, it is essential to remain longer in a positive state of mind where you are pretending that the miracle has already happened. To help you do this, I highly recommend expressive writing.

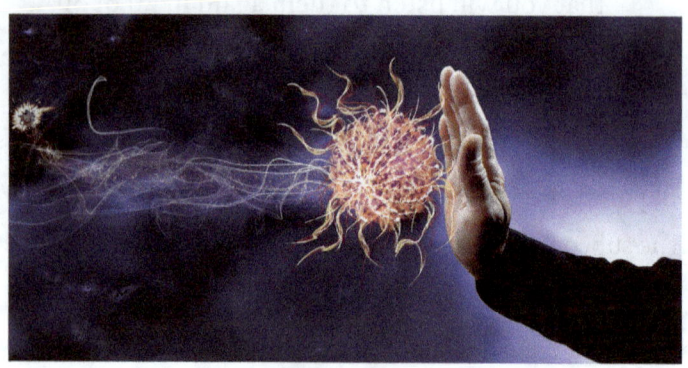

Bru-n0 [2]

Expressive Writing: A Secret Tool

To get rid of negative thought patterns, let go of the past, negative thoughts, feelings, pain, fear, etc:

- Grab plenty of paper and good pens. Find a place where you will be undisturbed for 15 to 20 minutes, then as fast as you can, write down all your hurt, pain, limiting thoughts, beliefs, feelings, etc. Nobody will ever read it, so it doesn't need to be legible.
- Getting this "stuff" out of your system is the key. Write until all of it is out and there is nothing more to write.
- Tear these pages apart in front of your eyes!
- Burn them, put them in a bin, or whatever other way you choose to get them out of your sight and out of your mind.
- You will notice that the more you do this, the easier it gets. Over time, you might even find that, in the end, you are writing solutions to your problems. These you can keep, of course.
- Do this every day for 30 days. After that, you will notice that it is easier to stay positive, and you will have less and less to write. Then, you might only do it every second day or so.

Expressive writing has been proven to help your brain disconnect from the problems and pain you have just written down. Although many studies show that it works, we cannot explain why. Please test it out for at least six weeks and see how it works for you. [4]

Remember, you are not alone in the process, so share your questions and inspirational changes on the Facebook page. This will motivate others to keep on going:
hypnosis-joondalup.com.au/
Unlock-the-Miracle-Within.

congerdesign [2]

johnhain [2]

Focus on uplifting thoughts and your positive future vision

Day-to-day living will bring challenges that distract you from your vision. So, how do you maintain uplifting thoughts and your positive vision for the future? What is the best way for you to change to a positive and uplifting mood?

You might already have some ideas, like listening to music, cuddling your pets, or enjoying an excellent, uplifting movie.

Here are some more suggestions:
- As you will have noticed already, the questions you ask yourself will impact your feelings. If you start and end your day with uplifting questions, it will be easier to keep working on the positive life changes that you are in the middle of now.
- Write down, or think about, 5 to 10 things that you are grateful for. They might be little things like a glass of fresh water or bigger things like your good health, the warmth of the shining sun, walking, etc. Can you feel the gratitude within you? Start and end your day with these 5 to 10 things in your mind, and feel the positive vibrations in your body.

Before you go to the next step, listen to and absorb the Hypnosis Session of Step 2.
https://hypnosis-joondalup.com.au/miracle-login/

Step 2 Hypnosis Session to internalise the truth about yourself

CHECKLIST

- [ ] **Listen to Miracle Question**
  Notes:
  _____
  _____

- [ ] **I have pretended the miracle has happened for ___ min / how many days?**
  Notes:
  _____
  _____

- [ ] **I have done expressive writing ___ times so far.**
  Notes:
  _____
  _____

- [ ] **Uplifting questions, gratitude:
  I am grateful for...**
  Notes:
  _____
  _____

- [ ] **What changes have you noticed so far?**
  Notes:
  _____
  _____

STEP TWO

The indisputable truth about you

You have already internalised the truth about yourself during the Step 2 Hypnosis Session, so this chapter will be easy for your subconscious mind to understand.

Unfortunately, when we are growing up, we are constantly comparing ourselves with others. Therefore, our society has a big problem: *I am not good enough!* Much of what we do is driven by this underlying feeling. Hence, we need a bigger or better car, a bigger, more expensive house... No matter what we do, buy, or earn, the deep inner emptiness is not filled. This is precisely why Step 2 is critical for your transformation.

The more unique something is, like a diamond or a

precious metal, the more expensive it is, right? Humans are probably the most complex beings on earth, and each is unique. So why don't we see each other as unique, precious, and beautiful?

AlainAudet [2]

Emotions can shape snowflakes and water

Have you ever seen pictures of snowflakes through a microscope? In the best-case scenario, those tiny white fluffy water drops have a life span of a few seconds to a few years.

UNLOCK THE MIRACLE WITHIN

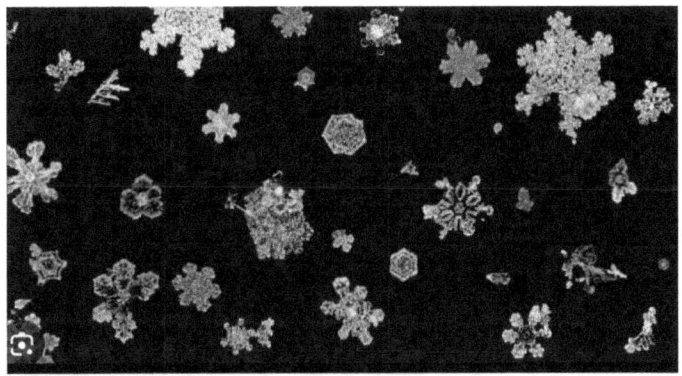

JillWellington [2]

Did you know that good emotions are needed to produce such beautiful shapes? Emotions and snowflakes? Yes, we will come back to this a little later.

If you google for more pictures of real snowflakes, you will see that – just like human beings – each snowflake is unique. Now, think briefly about how much creativity one must have to continuously create endless numbers of beautiful, unique snowflakes.

When you look closer, you will see that they all have six corners or edges. Which one is more beautiful than the other? The most common answer I get from my clients is: "That's hard to say." And this is the answer I am looking for!

Every one of those snowflakes is unique and beautiful. Whoever or whatever builds our world invests creativity, positive thoughts, and feelings into creating snowflakes.

Sounds strange? Feelings in creating snowflakes? Bear with me. I will explain this later in detail. The fact is that these beautiful snowflakes would not have been made without positive, good feelings. They would not look beautiful. Simple as that.

You might wonder, "How can love and positive emotions be seen in snowflakes?" Yes, indeed, emotions do affect water molecules!

Qimono [2]

Look at this "simple" glass of water. Dr Masaru Emoto's research on water demonstrates that emotions change the appearance of water molecules. Positive emotions like gratitude, peace and love create magnificent water crystals. Negative emotions do not create any crystals at all.

Watch this short video about the beauty of appreciation:

Go to the book member page: https://hypnosis-joondalup.com.au/miracle-login

OR go to hypnosis-joondalup.com.au/emotions-in-water. [5]

(6)

Can you see it? A positive, extraordinary, loving and imaginative force creates wonderfully. You are but one example of this!

Look at the snowflakes now: the universe's creative force designs each one! Each of them is unique, and created with positive energy reflected in their beauty.

It blows my mind that there is a creative force that loves creating beauty, and even puts good emotions into snowflakes that have a life span from a few seconds to perhaps a few years. What do you think? Is this not amazing?

Something as trivial as a snowflake is made with positive emotions, love, compassion, gratitude, truth, joy, harmony, and hope…. How many more positive thoughts and energy can be accumulated in a human being?

Have you listened to the related Hypnosis *Session* to internalise the truth about yourself? The indisputable truth about you is that you are gracefully and wonderfully made!

You are created "in the image of God".
You are God's highest creation!
The Course in Miracle Society says:
"I am as God created me". [7]
The Bible says: "So God created mankind
in his own image, in the image of God
he created them; male and female he
created them." [8] *God blessed them.*

Are you struggling to grasp that you are wonderfully made, loved, and blessed? You are not alone; our whole society is suffering from this. This is why I give this fridge magnet to my clients:

HOW TO DECEIVE YOUR SUBCONSCIOUS MIND INTO POSITIVITY

Here is a powerful exercise. Initially, your conscious mind will resist, but over time, your mind will accept this more and more.

- **Write positive, uplifting sentences like:**
  I am unique, I am wonderfully made
  I am gifted and talented
  I am beautiful
  I am smart
  I am kind
  I am ...
- **Place them all over your home, in your car, your phone, your screen saver – wherever you see them.**
  Put them in your bedroom, so that the first thing you see when opening your eyes in the morning and the last thoughts you read when you go to bed are uplifting and inspirational words. Write on your mirror so when you look at yourself subconsciously, you see yourself more and more in the loving eyes of your creator.

At first, you might feel some resistance, but you will gradually see yourself more and more as the unique and specially gifted person you are.

Imagine how your life will change as you change your thoughts about yourself and shift into positive expanding vibrations.

Human emotion can even be measured

How miraculous! Human emotion can not only be visualised in water crystals, it can also be measured! David Hawkins found a way to measure our emotions in electromagnetic waves.

Lower vibrations are contracting vibrations. You certainly have experienced this. You feel energised when you are with uplifting people; with depressed or depressed or angry people, you feel drained.

Some movies make you laugh, love and dream of a better world and future, while others make you feel anxious, angry, and filled with negative thoughts. It is strange, but in our society, it seems that negative emotions often have an addictive effect. Watch social media and the news: many items focus on negative information, war, accidents, bullying, and so on. As a result, our society is dragged down to negative energy, sucked into this destructive loop.

The more you become aware of your thoughts and feelings, the more you can take responsibility and choose how you will live your life. You will not be a victim because you can claim your power and decide to live a fulfilled life. After all, this is Your Life. You do have the right to be happy! Remember that you are unique, blessed and wonderfully made and nobody has the right to drag you down.

Imagine your new world

Just for a moment, imagine that you, your family, and your friends all feel blessed and loved. What if you left the house each morning feeling blessed and aiming to bless others? What if all the people around you did do the same?

What if you could uplift and motivate others to live their purpose and dreams as you do?

- How about you start your day by complimenting yourself on three things you can be happy or proud about?
- Then, on your way to work, is there somebody you can uplift by saying,
    - *I love your shoes*, or *Your hair looks fantastic*?
- Each person you meet at work is unique,

memorable, and beautiful. Open your eyes, detect their actual being, and find ways to compliment them with genuine, honest compliments.

Do this for a month, and you will be amazed at how you and your surroundings change. We all like to be seen, uplifted and complimented. After praising and congratulating yourself today, how many other people can you encourage?

The more you become aware of your emotions and how your environment, friends, social media, and TV impact them, the more you will consciously choose with whom you spend your time and the social media and TV you read, listen to, or watch. Your time and your emotional energy are precious, so use them wisely.

My personal experience with vibrations = emotions

For me, the easiest way to connect and feel closest to the light, the loving universal power, is to go camping. I go out into nature in a national park or a free campsite, where there is no internet, no control, no lights, hardly any people, just nature.

I can calm down and see the enormous, endless

heaven filled with shining, bright, inspirational stars. During the day, I am walking, marvelling at the blue sky, the birds singing in the trees, hearing my footsteps on the red soil... The Western Australian Outback fascinates me. I can easily imagine how the Aboriginals lived here, completely connected and as one with nature. There was no fear of not enough and no greed. It is easy to see that they often experienced harmony with each other, their gods and nature. I would love to learn more about their culture, not just from books and some guided tours.

Another way to picture human emotions

How Dr David Hawkins measured emotions

The Vibration Scale, also known as the Map of Consciousness, was developed by Dr David R Hawkins, a psychiatrist, spiritual teacher, and author of several books on spirituality and personal development. One of his most well-known works is *Power Vs. Force*.

The Vibration Scale is a hierarchical scale that assigns numerical values to various emotional states and levels of consciousness. The scale ranges from 20 at the bottom to 1000 at the top. Each level on the scale corresponds to a specific emotional state, thought pattern, or way of perceiving the world. The higher the level, the more positive and empowering the state of consciousness.

Here are some examples of emotional states and their corresponding positions on the Vibration Scale: [9]

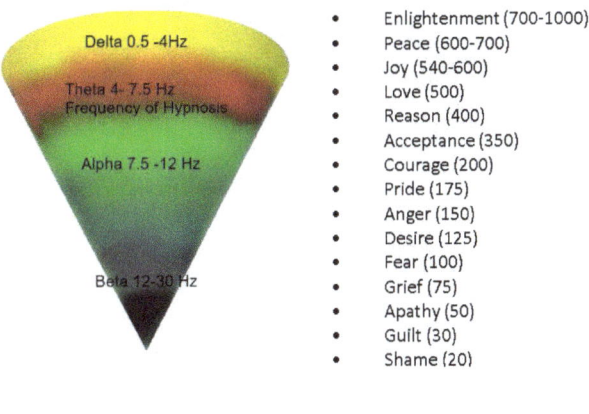

(10)

The Vibration Scale of Dr David Hawkins [11]

High levels of Beta waves (18-40 Hz) are associated with the less positive emotions of significant stress, anxiety and paranoia. [12]

As visualised in the research of Dr Masaru Emoto, water vibrates in different ways depending on different emotions. [13] How much water is in the human body?

- Brain and heart: 73% water
- Lungs: about 83% water
- Skin: 64% water
- Muscles and kidneys: 79% water.

Since your body is about 60% comprised of water, you also vibrate with emotions! It is vital to be able to change your vibrations into expanding energy. How do you do this? Start with loving yourself.

HOW TO LOVE YOURSELF: A STEP-BY-STEP GUIDE

Loving yourself is an essential aspect of overall well-being and personal growth. It will make forgiveness much more manageable. It's a process that involves self-acceptance, self-care, and a positive relationship with yourself.

Here are some steps you can take to cultivate self-love:
Practise Self-Compassion: Treat yourself with the kindness and understanding you would offer a friend. When facing challenges or setbacks, avoid self-criticism and replace it with self-compassion.

Positive Self-Talk: Monitor your inner dialogue. Replace negative self-talk with positive affirmations and statements acknowledging your strengths and accomplishments.

Embrace Your Uniqueness: Recognise that you are a unique individual with your own set of talents, qualities, and experiences. Embrace your differences and focus on your strengths.

Set Healthy Boundaries: Learn to say no when needed. Prioritise your well-being by setting boundaries that protect your time, energy, and emotions.

Practise Self-Care: Engage in activities that promote physical, emotional, and mental well-being. This could include exercise, mindfulness, reading, hobbies, or spending time with loved ones.

Forgive Yourself: Understand that everyone makes mistakes. Instead of dwelling on past errors, acknowledge them, learn from them, and then let them go.

Celebrate Your Achievements: Whether big or small, acknowledge your accomplishments. Celebrate your progress and the effort you put into reaching your goals.

Mindfulness and Meditation: Practising mindfulness and meditation can help you become more aware of your thoughts and feelings. This can lead to a deeper understanding of yourself and your emotions.

Surround Yourself with Positivity: Surround yourself with people who uplift and support you. Let go of relationships that drain your energy or bring negativity.

Focus on Personal Growth: Strive to learn and grow continually. Set goals that align with your interests and values, and work toward becoming the best version of yourself.

Accept Imperfections: Perfection is unattainable. Instead of striving for perfection, focus on progress and growth.

Practise Gratitude: Regularly take a moment to reflect on the things you're grateful for. This can help shift your perspective toward the positive aspects of your life.

Engage in Self-Reflection: Reflect on your thoughts, feelings, and experiences. Journalling can be a helpful tool for self-reflection.

Seek Professional Help: If you struggle with self-love due to deep-seated issues or mental health challenges, consider seeking support from a therapist or counsellor.

Remember that self-love is a journey, and it's okay to have ups and downs. It's a continuous process of learning, growing, and nurturing a positive relationship with yourself. Be patient with yourself and celebrate the progress you make along the way.

Step 2 is a critical step to finding your life's purpose. In Step 3, we will address the "programs" in your mind that stop you from being the best you can be: blocks, past beliefs, programming from your childhood, and the hurts and pains that hinder you from moving forward.

This journey is not a race, so take all the time you need for each step. Be kind to yourself and listen to your inner voice. Learn to trust your inner voice more and more, the voice that means well for you, the uplifting, encouraging voice. This voice is the one that knows the truth about you, and that you are unique, loved, gifted and talented.

SUMMARY

The indisputable truth about you is that you are gracefully and wonderfully made. You are good enough!

Beautiful emotions create beautiful ice crystals. Beautiful emotions create the universe and you.

Positive emotions are expanding vibrations. The more you can tune in to positive thoughts and feelings about yourself, the calmer and more relaxed you will be, and you will become more aware of who and what is good for you and what is not.

Here is your link again:
https://hypnosis-joondalup.com.au/miracle-login

HYPNOSIS SESSION REVIEW

How often have you listened to the Hypnosis Session that guides you through this to internalise this?
_____
_____

What makes this easy, and what makes it challenging to grasp this concept?
_____
_____

Do you have uplifting statements all over your house and your mirror?
_____
_____

Ideas for how to improve this further:
_____
_____

How aware are you of your vibrations?
_____
_____

How is the step-by-step guide to self-love helping you?
_____
_____

STEP 3

Let go of your past and be free to live as you

How did you go with Steps 1 and 2? They were the ideal preparation for the next phase. Are you feeling more content with yourself, calmer, more at peace? The more you have adopted the previous transformational changes, the more effortless your journey through the following chapters will be.

The further you are along in this workbook, the more at peace you will feel. You will be more conscious of your inner voices, and you will be better and better equipped to deal with the negative voices. As you realise that they are not telling you the truth about yourself, it will become easier to stop them. The more you are in tune with your true self, that magnificent and fantastic human being you are, the more you will unlock your potential and live to fulfil it.

Geralt [2]

Keep going. My hypnosis clients have used these 5 Steps to turn their lives around and set themselves free from past limiting beliefs, hurts and pains. This chapter will guide you further along your way to healing and being free from any negative thoughts you or somebody else has put into your mind.

By now, you are aware of the two voices in your head and the feelings in your body. How wonderful would it be to clearly state that one voice is from your past and has nothing more to do with here and now, and only take the uplifting voice seriously?

This is your life. You are unique. The more you live your true purpose and passion, the more fulfilled your life will become.

Step 3 will guide you through a process to heighten your awareness about your own limiting thoughts, beliefs, rules, and anything you feel you must do that makes sense for your future.

URSULA D. KNECHT

Bessi [2]

Babies and toddlers are like sponges, absorbing the information that comes to them from the environment. No filter tells them this is good, learn this, and this is bad, and do not believe this is true. Further, babies, toddlers, and kids up to the age of about 13 are excellent observers. They learn to adapt to "acceptable" behaviours. It is even more essential for kids to "belong" than it is for adults. This is a simple survival instinct. The one that fits in best has the highest chance of being treated better, receiving favours and surviving.

This continues into adulthood. We are dependent on each other. We all need a home and a workplace where we are accepted. So it is normal to have a subconscious fear of abandonment. And sometimes, the fear of abandonment and being disconnected from the people around us leads us to do things that are not good for us.

The struggle comes when the outside world and the inside world collide. What happens when you do not listen to your inner voice and instead make a decision that conflicts with your heart and feelings? Let me tell you about a time that this happened to me.

In my early 30s, I probably made my worst ever decision! I had chosen a very narrow-minded peer group. Perhaps it was just because my friends weren't there and I was seeking guidance. An intolerant group tells you precisely what is right and what is wrong. There is no compassion or love, just black and white.

When my best friend got married, I had a void to fill. Afraid of ending up lonely, I got a boyfriend. He was pretty lovely and went to a similar church to mine. From the outside, we made a perfect picture and married. As soon as we lived together, the problems started. We went to therapy, but we could not find each other.

I had never felt so lonely and so abandoned. I never felt good enough; there was no love, only demands. I felt so empty inside, and a deep sadness overcame me. It felt as if all joy in life had left me, and the world around me became darker and darker. The doctor prescribed anti-depressant medication, not that I felt any different with them. I did my best to pretend to be OK over Christmas while dwelling on how to end my life. What held me back was that I did not want to hurt my mum, who had always loved me very much, no matter what I did.

Then New Year's Eve came, and I felt a burst of self-preserving energy soaring within me. I decided to live again. I chose to live on my terms, breaking free from this bondage to seek happiness again and be me.

I was ready to meet new people and make new friends. I was ready, so the universe delivered. I started to form beautiful friendships away from my church. I was living again, despite my whole house of cards falling to pieces and "my" church condemning me for leaving my husband.

Yes, listening to your inner, caring voice can be very challenging. It might mean finding new friends, a new job, or changing your environment. Trust me; I don't regret the challenges I had to endure, as they shaped me into the person I am today.

Many challenges in my life have taken me through persistently confronting times. Eventually, after years of therapy and learning, I could forgive those who hurt me and took advantage of me. I also realised that without these experiences, I would not have become compassionate and understanding of other people's limitations, sadness and pain.

Empower the positive feelings in your mind and body

Are you listening to your inner voices? What do they say? You can use your body to assess your feelings. Usually, the truth feels light, and lies feel heavy.

Pretend for a moment that you are relaxing in a comfortable chair and listening to my voice as if you were a client in my hypnosis room.

- When you feel sad, stressed or anxious (your negative feeling), where in your body is this feeling? What colour does it have? What shape and size? Is this feeling moving or still? Does it have any taste or smell?

Fantastic, you are doing just fine. Yes, indeed, you are doing great.

- Now, while you are here in this safe, relaxing place, think of 3 to 5 uplifting situations where you have felt marvellous. Tune into these positive feelings. Where do you feel them in your body? What colour, what shape? Taste? Smell? Can you make the positive feelings bigger, even filling your whole body with them?

Some clients cannot make the good feelings bigger or brighter before the hypnosis session. If this sounds like you, you can make your positive feelings more colourful and vivid by listening to the *Step 2 Hypnosis Session to internalise the truth about yourself.*

Here is where to find it:
https://hypnosis-joondalup.com.au/miracle-login

Listen to your inner voices – feel your emotions

The Step 2 Hypnosis Session will empower you to connect to your positive feelings and listen to your voices. But sometimes, an inner negative emotion might be there to protect you. Feel and listen carefully; usually, the lighter sense tells you the truth. The more you can objectively look from the outside, and feel and hear your inner voice, the more easily you can find guidance.

If you feel your negative voices overwhelm you at any stage, seek help, talk to a friend, or do the expressive writing exercise, and lift yourself with one of the earlier hypnosis sessions.

How can you evolve through changing shape? Literally!

Opal [2]

I love to see butterflies' beauty and grace as they are effortlessly flying through the air. But to become such graceful insects, they go through strenuous transformations.

In each stage of the butterfly's life, although there is no change in their DNA, their shape and lifestyle are transformed. They start from eggs to become continuously feeding and crawling caterpillars, then restful pupas, and finally graceful butterflies. This fantastic insect goes through a complete transformation, which is called metamorphosis. [14]

Imagine how caterpillars think and feel when they eat constantly and crawl from leaf to leaf. They may just focus on the next leaf to eat, with no idea about the beauty and greatness inside them. How will it feel to slowly and patiently break free from this pupa, unfolding those enormous, beautiful wings and then fly away?

I am astonished by these mesmerising metamorphic changes. How does the creator make such marvellous transformational changes possible? And how do these little creatures know how to fly without ever learning it?

Could this be a metaphor for your life? At what stage in your life are you? Your DNA also does not change through all the transformations you are experiencing. Where are you now, and how do you want to spread your wings in the future?

What if you could let go of everything that stops you from spreading your wings and fly into a new life? What would you do? Where would you go? With whom would you want to share your life?

Do the Miracle Meditation again. What do you see and experience this time? Do you see a brighter, more colourful future with more possibilities? If you are reading this book while you are in a crisis, it might clarify some steps for you and help you make good decisions. Even David in the Bible went through dark valleys and problems.

Even though I walk through the valley of the shadow of death, I will fear no evil, for you are with me; your rod and your staff comfort me.
PSALM 23:4 [15]

We all go through valleys of darkness, asking questions and standing before closed doors; that is part of life. At these times, it is very comforting to believe in something bigger than you. It is never easy, and sometimes a crisis can seem never-ending. If you feel this way, please seek help. There is light at the end of the tunnel.

Never judge a book by its cover

Even when you feel alone with your problems, people around you might have similar issues. When you look at people from the outside, they are often not what you think.

> I have had to learn this several times in my life. The most profound experience was waiting in the hospital for radiation therapy to combat my breast cancer. All the people sitting in the waiting room were there for radiation therapy, so we were on the journey together.
>
> Many looked well from the outside, with no sign of the challenges they faced. In contrast, I had lost my hair. We were not focused on our phones, as happens in many other waiting rooms. We talked to each other. Further, we talked about life, and most of the time, we spoke of uplifting and encouraging topics. Most of these people were looking well from

the outside, but they had cancer. I learned not to judge people by their outside appearances.

Never think you know what people are going through in their lives. Give them the benefit of the doubt and excuse them if they are unfriendly to you.

Turn away from darkness and look into light and hope

Jplenio [2]

When you are facing a challenge like cancer, your life experiences can suddenly change. Life no longer seems endless, and you can't take life for granted. Moreover, you find yourself looking at life from a different place.

What changes would you make if you realised deep inside that you could no longer take life for granted? How would your priorities shift?

What would urgently become vital to you? What lifestyle changes would you make? What gifts and talents have you been hiding from the world so far? Would you share them with the world now, without fear of failure? Here are two critical questions to consider:

- What rules, behaviours, and beliefs have you learned in childhood and adulthood?
- Which of them are still helping you, and which are hindering you?

What do you say to yourself?

Your self-talk reveals your thoughts about yourself. You will see that the more aware you become of your self-talk, the more closely you will listen to what others say.

Here is an example of a limiting belief. A new client came to see me in my physio clinic for his chronic lower back pain. He stated: "You cannot help me." What was his belief? Perhaps he had been disappointed many times, and nothing had changed. What would your response have been?

This client had seen many physios before me, and it seemed they had tried to convince him that they could help him. So what did I say? "Yes, you are right." His inner belief was that there was no hope and nobody could help him. And I knew very well that even the best therapist cannot help someone who does not want to help themselves.

Do you have ingrained beliefs that stop you from moving forward? Can you see yourself in statements like this:

- *I will never be able to do this.*
- *This pain will never ease.*
- *I will never find a soul mate.*
- *I will never be out of debt.*
- *I will never...*

By now, I hope you are becoming more and more aware of your negative self-talk. Here is a simple way to change it:

- Instead of saying: *I can't do this!* Say: *I do not know yet how to do this.*
- Instead of saying: *I tried already many times and failed; I give up!* Say: *I am doing my best and will eventually find a way to make this happen.*

Do you know the story of Thomas Edison, who invented the light bulb?

> *As an inventor, Edison made 1,000 unsuccessful attempts at inventing the light bulb. A reporter asked, "How did it feel to fail 1,000 times?" Edison replied, "I didn't fail 1,000 times. The light bulb was an invention with 1,000 steps."* [16]

Do you still live by rules you learned in your childhood that no longer benefit you? Does your family or the environment you grew up in have specific rules or culture that you could easily change, and improve your life?

Our childhood's rules, beliefs, and behaviours have much to do with the culture and country we are growing up in, our family's social status, and religion.

> I grew up in Switzerland and now live in Australia. In Switzerland, people speak their minds and tell you what they think about a topic, even if you don't want to know it. Swiss people often talk over the top of each other, and this is normal.
>
> In Australia, I find it hard to know what people think. It is also considered impolite to interrupt someone who is speaking. The cultural differences between Australia and Switzerland are relatively small, but they benefit me, as they make me aware of my culture and the differences.

Your cultural background tells you what to believe about women and men, and what "good" relationships are or are not. You learn what is right and what is wrong. However, if you look closely, travel the world, read books, and learn about other cultures and ways of living, you will see that few rules are truly black and white.

Therefore, it is worthwhile to look at your own life and decide consciously what rules make sense for you now, and which ones do not. The challenge is, how flexible are you? Are you willing to change your rules if they do not make any sense anymore? My partner and I had decided that Daisy, our cat, would not be allowed in the bedroom, yet it took only a few days, and Daisy slept on our bed 😊.

Can you laugh at yourself? Life is so much easier if you don't take yourself too seriously, and you can laugh about your mistakes. It helps you to move on quickly, without wasting energy dwelling on your mistakes. Edison did not waste time beating himself up and having negative thoughts about himself that he had still not succeeded. He learned from each step that did not yet work, and finally got that light to shine. He moved on every day. Every day, Edison told himself he had found another way that this was not working; therefore, he had to be closer to finding out how it would work.

The more you become aware of what you say to yourself and other people, the more you become aware of what others say to themselves. You will be surprised about your own and your friends' limiting beliefs. How often do we hear people saying:

> *No, we can't do that.*
> *No, we can't afford it.*
> *No, we can't.*
> *We don't have enough money to do that.*
> *Now, that's too expensive!*
> *I'm not smart enough to do that.*
> *I cannot study.*
> *I don't have a degree...*

Do these ways of thinking and these limiting beliefs hold you back? The following exercise might help you.

WHAT WOULD IT TAKE TO FIND BETTER ANSWERS EVERY DAY?

Below, on the left are your limiting negative thoughts, and on the right are the positive answers you give yourself. I have given some examples. In the spaces, write down your own thoughts.

I am not smart enough to...?	*I can learn whatever I put my mind to.*
I cannot afford this.	*I will find a way to afford this.*
I will not find a job.	*The right job is waiting for me.*
I will never find a soul mate.	*The more I become a better person, the more I will attract my soul mate / ideal business partner...*
I will never be able to let go of my past.	*The more I focus on gratefulness and a bright future, the easier I can leave my past behind.*

_____

_____

_____

_____

_____

_____

Now, ask these questions about each item you have written:

OK, where did that belief come from?
Is that because my mum said that?
Is that because my dad said that?
Is this because I experienced that?
What kind of thinking process is behind that?

ColiNOOB [2]

On this journey to your true inner self, you are getting closer to choosing your life the way you want. You can also look at yourself in love and with compassion and ask yourself, *Who am I?* And just when you thought you had dealt with your past, this nagging self-doubt and that sinking feeling of not good enough surges again.

Words are powerful!

Geralt [2]

Freeing yourself from limiting beliefs is a decisive step towards personal growth and achieving your full potential. Here is a guide to identifying and overcoming these beliefs:

A PROCESS TO FREE YOURSELF FROM LIMITING BELIEFS

1. **Identify Limiting Beliefs.** Start by becoming aware of the beliefs that hold you back. These negative thoughts often undermine your self-confidence, worth, and abilities. As these beliefs come to mind, write them down.
2. **Question Their Validity.** Examine each limiting belief critically. Ask yourself:
   - Where did this belief come from?
   - Is there any evidence to support it?
   - Have I tested or challenged this belief before?
     - Does this belief align with my values and goals?
3. **Replace Them with Empowering Beliefs.** Counteract each limiting belief with a positive and empowering one. For example, if your limiting view is: "I'm not smart enough to succeed", replace it with "I am capable of learning and growing, and I can succeed through effort and dedication."
4. **Gather Contradictory Evidence.** Collect examples from your life where you've proven

your limiting beliefs were wrong. These instances show that your beliefs are not absolute truths.

5. **Visualise Success.** Use visualisation techniques to imagine yourself succeeding despite your past beliefs. Visualising success can help rewire your brain to focus on positive outcomes.

6. **Affirmations.** Practise affirmations daily. Affirmations are positive statements that reinforce your new empowering beliefs. Repeat them with conviction and confidence in their truth.

7. **Challenge Negative Self-Talk.** Pay attention to your internal dialogue. Whenever you think or say something negative about yourself, challenge it by asking for evidence or replacing it with a positive thought.

8. **Seek Support.** Share your journey with friends, family, or a therapist. They can provide encouragement and perspective and help you stay accountable for your progress.

9. **Continuous Self-Reflection.** Regularly check in with yourself. Reflect on your progress and identify any lingering limiting beliefs that need further attention.

10. **Take Action.** Actively challenge your comfort zone. Engage in activities that align with your new empowering beliefs, and celebrate your achievements along the way.
11. **Practise Patience.** Overcoming limiting beliefs is a gradual process. Be patient and understand that it takes time to rewire your thought patterns.
12. **Cultivate Self-Compassion.** Treat yourself kindly throughout this process. Remember that everyone has limiting beliefs; working on them shows strength and growth.

Remember, changing beliefs is a journey that requires consistent effort and self-awareness. It's about transforming your mindset to align with your goals and aspirations. Celebrate your progress and acknowledge each step you take towards a more positive and empowered way of thinking.

Make peace with your past

Forgiveness – how to let go of past hurt and pain

To live your life free from the past and discover your full potential is a vital step. Forgiveness does not mean that what happened to you is OK, but it is the only way the perpetrators no longer have any power over you.

Negative vibrations hold you down in a contracting, energetic state. If you feel shame (20), guilt (30), apathy (50), grief (75) or fear (100), you are living in suffering. Negative vibrations keep your suffering going. To live a fulfilled life, you must let go of them. As long as these feelings have you feeling like a victim and suffering, your offenders will still have power over your life. Please do not give your perpetrators any more time, thoughts, and energy in your life. Choose to be free!

Set yourself free – TODAY!

4653867 [2]

As with the previous steps, forgiveness can be easier to achieve in hypnosis than with your conscious mind. Why is this?

In my hypnosis sessions, you go to a beautiful, peaceful, safe place. You will be filled with light and surrounded by angels of wisdom and love.

In this peaceful state, filled with love and wisdom, your subconscious mind finds a way to forgive. Your subconscious mind wants the best for you, and has wanted you to heal and be set free for years.

Therefore, you might have to listen several times to the recorded hypnosis session on forgiveness (*Step 3 – Hypnosis to make peace with your past – Forgiveness*). That is OK. The good thing is that you now have a tool in your toolbox to deal with these negative feelings when they come up again.

In combination with this recording, expressive writing can also be supportive. If the hurt is deep and persistent, consider seeking additional help from a counsellor or psychologist.

Please do not skip this step. It is likely the most essential part of this process. Forgiveness is your pathway to a brighter future. There is no shortcut.

By cutting all cords to your past, you are freeing yourself to move forward.

Myriams-Fotos (2)

I would expect this chapter to trigger memories and negative emotions for you. Please be kind to yourself. To begin with, start the forgiveness process with people or situations that are easier. Take your time, do not pressure yourself, tune in to yourself and feel which topic, person, or situation is next on the list.

You do not have to have this all sorted and finalised before you move on to Step 4. However, it is essential to have started it.

Use your expressive writing tool to remove those negative feelings from your system. Throw them away. Then, immerse yourself in the hypnosis session for forgiveness (Step 3 – Hypnosis to make peace with your past – Forgiveness).

Be patient. This will take time, even with hypnosis. Depending on your situation and personality, you might find it easier to forgive others but harder to forgive yourself, or vice versa. Just be patient with yourself and take one step at a time. Take the time to return to previous sessions where you can enhance your self-love and patience.

Letting go of past hurt and pain through forgiveness can be a challenging but ultimately liberating process. This journey guides you to your inner balance.

hallok (2)

SUMMARY

There are many ways to navigate this journey. In addition to the hypnosis session on forgiveness, you might choose this process to guide you more consciously:

Acknowledge Your Feelings: Recognise and accept the emotions you're experiencing due to the past hurt. It's okay to feel anger, sadness, or frustration. Acknowledging these emotions is the first step towards healing.

Understand the Impact: Reflect on how holding onto the pain affects your emotional well-being, relationships, and overall quality of life. Recognising the negative impact can motivate you to seek healing and change.

Shift Perspective: Try to view the situation from a different angle. This doesn't mean justifying the hurtful actions, but seeking to understand the circumstances that might have led to them. This perspective shift can help foster empathy.

Practise Self-Compassion: Treat yourself with kindness and understanding. Understand that you deserve to heal and move forward healthily. Self-compassion is a vital aspect of forgiveness.

Choose Forgiveness: Forgiveness is a conscious decision. Choose to release the grip of resentment and the desire for revenge. This decision empowers you to regain control over your emotions.

Write a Letter (Optional): Consider writing a letter to the person who hurt you, even if you don't intend to send it. Express your feelings and thoughts in a safe space. This exercise can be cathartic and aid in processing emotions. Or use expressive writing.

Set Boundaries: If the person who hurt you is still in your life, establish clear boundaries to protect yourself from further harm. Boundaries help maintain your emotional well-being.

Practise Empathy: Empathy doesn't excuse hurtful actions but can help you understand that people are complex and flawed. This understanding can contribute to your healing process.

Release Resentment: As you work through your emotions, make a conscious effort to release resentment. This might require repeated reminders that in continuing to hold resentment, you're choosing to let go of your well-being.

Focus on Healing: Engage in activities that bring you joy, whether spending time with loved ones, pursuing hobbies, exercising, or practising mindfulness. Focusing on positive experiences can aid in your healing journey.

Seek Support: If the hurt is deep and persistent, consider seeking support from a therapist, counsellor, or support group. They can provide guidance tailored to your situation.

Patience and Time: Healing and forgiveness take time. Be patient with yourself. It's okay to have moments of regression, but continue to work towards emotional freedom.

Forgiveness is a Personal Journey: There's no set timeline for achieving forgiveness. The goal is to release the burden of the past and create space for healing, growth, and a more peaceful future.

Please take your time for Step 3. It is critical to find your peace.

NoName_13 [2]

CHECKLIST

Write down your thoughts and feelings about these steps:

Empower your mind and body with your positive feelings.
Notes:
_____
_____

Listen to your inner voices – feel your emotions.
Notes:
_____
_____

Turn around and look into the light and hope
Notes:
_____
_____

What would it take to find better answers daily?
Notes:
_____
_____

The process to free yourself from limiting beliefs:
Notes:
_____
_____

- **Make peace with your past**
  Notes:
  _____
  _____

- **Forgiveness – how to let go of past hurt and pain**
  Notes:
  _____
  _____

- **How to love yourself- a process to reinforce previous changes**
  Notes:
  _____
  _____

- **The Journey to Forgiveness**
  Notes:
  _____
  _____

STEP 4

Discover your hidden potential

Congratulations on reaching this part of your journey to unlock your hidden potential. Like the warmth of spring after the cold of winter, this chapter is your new awakening. No matter how long winter is, spring always follows. Nature illustrates what is waiting for us so wonderfully. When we have let go of last year's leaves, flowers and fruit, we are ready for new life. Spring is a fascinating time of the year. There is a new awakening, fresh life energy, creativity, and abundant life everywhere you look. I love the spring here in our Australian bush.

Ursula Knecht

You have gone through the previous steps, from autumn to winter. Now you are ready for spring, with its new ideas, life, opportunities, and doors to open. You have chosen to let go of the leaves from last season and now you may move forward freely.

I wonder how your imagination and future vision have changed since you started this book, with the Miracle Question. When you repeat the Miracle Question now, what are you dreaming of? Now that you are free, what path do you choose? What are you ready to experience? Are there countries you want to explore? Subjects you want to study? What skills do you want to enhance?

In the Hypnosis Session called *Discover Your Hidden Garden*, your subconscious mind will find even more answers. The journey will guide your subconscious mind to a hidden, abundant, forgotten garden. Every time you visit this garden, it will grow more and more beautiful, more and more alive, vivid, flowering and fruitful. Your creativity will expand endlessly, and your garden will be beautiful and abundant.

Your subconscious mind will guide you through this awakening. You might not see much evidence as the journey begins, but keep your future vision, dreams, and imagination going. Pretend they are already happening. The positive energy, thoughts and vibration you put into your future vision will make them happen.

Here is where to find the Hypnosis Session:
https://hypnosis-joondalup.com.au/miracle-login

Step 4 The Hidden Garden Hypnosis - Discover your hidden potential.

HOW TO VISUALISE YOUR FUTURE

Use the *Discover Your Hidden Garden* hypnosis to open your mind and dream of your ideal future.

- Write your future vision in the present tense as if it is already here.
- Now create a vision board, to support your subconscious mind as it envisions your future dreams and goals. A vision board is a wall you decorate with pictures showing your vision. This might be your dream house, soul mate, annual earnings, or award you want to achieve... whatever you see in your own vision for the future.
- Another option is to put your pictures into a vision book and look through them in the morning and again in the evening before bed.
- To make your transformation as effortless as possible, use the tools you already know, such as the *Miracle Question* and the *Discover Your Hidden Garden*.
  Dreams are the seedlings of reality. [1]

UNLOCK THE MIRACLE WITHIN

Paul_Stachowiak [2]

Discover Your Hidden Potential is perhaps the most comforting chapter in this book. Take your time in this part of the process, and then you will be ready for the final chapter on living your life on your terms.

You have done a fantastic job learning to listen to your inner voices, understanding which one benefits and uplifts you, and which one drags you down. You have opened your mind to two new possibilities, letting go of many familiar but restricting thoughts and beliefs and setting yourself free for a new year, as Mother Nature does each year in spring.

Now you have experienced the *Discover Your Hidden Garden* hypnosis session and are beginning to discover your hidden potential. You feel that your self-love is growing more and more. You are becoming calmer, content, relaxed, and at ease.

You are open to new thoughts, points of view and possibilities and have an open mind. And can see yourself doing something new and behaving in different ways than before. You're not just starting a new chapter in your life. You're starting a new year – your new life, your spring.

You are now asking yourself much better questions, leading you to find answers to what you seek. What would it take to find my soul mate? How can I find my ideal profession, a job where I love working with passion? How would it feel to have my own business? What steps would I have to take?

You have found the truth about yourself. Are you ready to live your purpose and enjoy a prosperous, full and happy life?

Why abandon a superbly running business? (Part 2)

The fire walk had transformed our lives. Marianne and I had been running in the hamster wheel. I had been working 70 hours a week. I had lost the spark in my life, and finding it again was a goal to strive for. The seminar kindled a new desire for change in me.

Australia! Marianne had never even been there before. And neither she nor I spoke fluent English. In my travels through Australia in 1996, I fell in love with this vast continent and the open-hearted people. I even experienced a culture shock when I went back to Switzerland.

Dreaming of Australia, showing Marianne all the pictures I had taken in 1996, and watching movies and documentaries about Australia was the first step. But, moving to Australia, the other end of the world? We knew that we did not speak good enough English. We had a dream but no idea how to make it a reality.

We attended an information session about immigrating to Australia. Fortunately, the lady sharing the information with us spoke German. She informed us that for Marianne, as a nurse, it would be pretty easy to get a visa. However, it would be challenging for me. First, physiotherapists were not on the skilled immigration list. Second, I would not be considered a partner for the current visa requirements. However, she said that visa requirements constantly change, so we should start with studying English and then see what visas were offered after we passed the English exams.

Sometimes in life, it is better not to know what hurdles come ahead, and just focus on your dreams.

A BURNING DESIRE TO BE, AND TO DO
is the starting point from which
the dreamer must take off.[1]

Exactly! Never stop dreaming. Don't give up when you are facing hurdles or setbacks.

The hurdles and challenges

It is much easier to face and overcome challenges if you have a partner at your side. This might be your business partner, best friend or soul mate. Fortunately, I was not alone. Marianne and I kept the dream alive together. We studied English, listened to BBC radio and watched as much TV in English as we could (it is much easier nowadays than it was then).

We saved four weeks of holidays, went to England, and intensively invested in our English, to get up to the required IELTS score. Additionally, I spent days on the immigration webpage, finding all the bits and pieces, and learning which visa to apply for. At that time, it was a very poorly designed website, and a daunting job to do by myself.

Hurdle One:
Our English teacher was amazed that Marianne passed the English test; but I struggled with it. Years ago, my schoolteachers had been clear about my language skills: "Just not talented!" My subconscious programming blocked me, and I repeatedly failed English exams. Thus, it took me ages to finally be accepted at Uni.

What subconscious programs do you have that hinder you to succeed? Now I know how fast these programs can be transformed with hypnosis!

For a while, there was the option that I could be accepted as a partner to immigrate to Australia, and we applied for a partner visa for me. But it was not long before the full package was returned by post. The visa requirements had just changed, and I was not accepted as Marianne's partner.

I sent in the next visa application for Marianne, this time with all the details separate from mine. I would go to Australia as an International Student.

Keep your dream alive - keep visualising your future!

Hurdle Two:
During all these challenges, we kept visualising our future in Australia. It is interesting to look and see that we never discussed giving up on our dream. We had no idea how long it would take and what hurdles we had to conquer along the way.

Follow the journey of others and learn from it:
We wanted to avoid as many mistakes as possible, so we watched a TV series about people moving to other countries to see their challenges and mistakes. I see no need to make the same mistakes others have made beforehand.

Visualise and talk about your ideal future:
We also watched all available movies and documentaries about Australia and had pictures of Australia hanging on our walls. We spoke to each other about going to Australia. We were dreaming of Australia, a permanent residency visa...

Eventually, the visa came through in 2006 – four years after our visualisation session – for Marianne. But not for me! I applied for an international student visa.

Further challenges:
We arrived in Australia. It was a tough first year of cultural shock, struggles, and not understanding enough English while studying seven days a week. But I finally passed the English test and then the Master of Sports Physiotherapy at Curtin University, Western Australia.

We had a special way to visualise our future and achieve our goal:
Most mornings, Marianne and I ran along the Swan River in the Perth's Victoria Gardens, through a memorial park with several stones. Each stone represented for us another hurdle, another exam.

We visualised that each stone was just a test along the way and that I would get a visa to stay. Each time we arrived at the last one, we cheered and congratulated each other for achieving the goal, as if we had already earned it.

Ursula Knecht

Towards the end of 2007, the expiration date of my student visa came closer and closer. It was just two weeks before my visa was to expire when Marianne happened to be looking up something for her nursing studies, and found that the visa requirement had changed again. Now, I would be accepted as her partner. Yeah! It was literally the last minute. We could stay in Australia – a dream five years in the making finally came true! Sometimes, the universe works in mysterious ways.

Now it is your turn! Make your dreams come true!

fancycravel [2]

Another Crucial Key to Achieving Your Goals

Asking better questions opens your world to new possibilities

The voices in your mind are linked directly to the questions you are asking yourself. You can ask yourself deflating, frustrating questions, or energising and inspirational questions.

Remember the story of Thomas Edison? When the reporter asked how it felt to fail 1,000 times, Edison's reply revealed a great deal about his thoughts about himself and his effort in inventing the light bulb. He said, *"I didn't fail 1,000 times. The light bulb was an invention with 1,000 steps."* [16]

If Edison's self-talk had been negative and frustrating, would he ever have invented the light bulb? Imagine the questions he would have asked himself. He just trusted that with every attempt that did not work, he would automatically come closer to eventually succeeding. What do you say to yourself when you hit a roadblock?

And suddenly, life stops – all travel plans are thrown overboard

How can you ever be prepared when the unexpected happens? You never want to get this phone call after a routine mammogram. What do you think when they call you up, saying you URGENTLY have to go to the hospital for a more detailed picture? What do you do?

"OK, I will come on Thursday morning. But we have plans to fly to Switzerland later the same day," I replied.

Denial. It can't be. I have a healthy lifestyle, regular exercise, and healthy diet. It can only be that they need better pictures. Let's pack and expect to fly to Switzerland. Let's hope for the best!

However, it still hits hard even if you try to prepare yourself for bad news. Surgery in two weeks. Then chemo and radiation... the complete program. Marianne was even more shocked than I was when we had to cancel our travel plans to see family in Switzerland.

I don't want to go into detail. This book is not about my cancer, nor is it about me. I want my stories to inspire you to keep living your life, no matter what. I offer my own experience to illustrate how the mindset works when life happens.

What would you do? How would you manage the situation? What can you learn from my stories?

Surprisingly, I dealt with the situation quite calmly after the first shock. I just accepted it and focused on making the best out of it. Somehow, I was able to use all my years of personal development to help me focus on what I could do and not what I could not do. I focused on healing. I knew my immune system would work better if I was in a good mood, loving, and trusting in the universe's guidance. I knew that worrying about it would not help.

In my self-reflection, I concluded my cancer was due to stress and worry. I did not want to add more of that - I wanted to live. I felt profoundly that I needed to relax, enjoy daily life and trust the universe.

Are you worrying about things out of your control? STOP now!

The surgery was booked. It was two weeks away, and we already had some holiday planned anyway. It was the beautiful wildflower season in Western Australia, so we went camping.

Ursula Knecht

As I was walking through colourful fields of wildflowers, I imagined that the vibration of the flowers would heal me. I was completely present, immersed in nature's beauty and relaxing, being at one with creation.

Every day, I meditated. Whenever worries came up, I stopped them. I decided that I would do whatever it takes to live! Fears and worries had no place in my mind anymore.

You have dealt with controlling your thoughts and emotions in previous steps. How well are you going with it? Remember that this is a continuous journey, and we must be patient with ourselves. But we also to be firm with the voice that hinders us from being our best selves.

Surprisingly, when the surgery came, the cancer was smaller than they had expected from the mammogram taken two weeks earlier. Also, It was capsuled in so it could not spread further.

How grateful I was that it seemed better than predicted! Perhaps my meditation and prayers had helped.

Choose your thoughts wisely – they can be life-changing

Remember the gratitude exercise in Step One? How well are you changing your thoughts and feelings when they turn negative? What strategies work best for you?

Please share them on the Facebook page:
https://hypnosis-joondalup.com.au/Unlock-the-Miracle-Within

We are all on our way in this journey of life. The more strategies we have in our toolbox, the more easily we will manage times of struggle.

CHECKLIST

Write down your thoughts and feelings about:

The Hidden Garden Hypnosis Session - Discover your hidden potential.
Notes:
_____
_____
_____

Asking better questions opens your world to new possibilities.
Notes:
_____
_____
_____

Your thoughts can be life-changing! Choose them wisely!
Notes:
_____
_____
_____

STEP 5

Live your life on your terms

How exciting! Now you can decide what is important to you, and how you want to live your life. This step will guide you to define your life and what is essential to you.

Decide to live your life on your terms. This is the most exciting Step. Why not just start with this Step and skip the previous four? You will know why if you have worked through the first four Steps. You are not the same person as you were when you started this process. Skipping the previous steps would not have freed you to choose the essence of your being.

Remember, spring always follows winter. The previous steps have guided you to this final one. You can now decide who you want to become, how you want to prioritise your life, and what values you want to strive for.

Step 5 has four parts:
1. Defining Your Values
2. Life Balance
3. The 80/20 Rule
4. Goal Setting

For this step to be most effective, I recommend reading one part, doing the hypnosis session, reading the next part and, repeating the hypnosis session, and so on. This way, you will see how you can visualise and set more inspirational goals.

https://hypnosis-joondalup.com.au/miracle-login/

Step 5 Hypnosis for Future Vision and Goal Setting

Please share your journey and ask some questions to the related Facebook group

https://hypnosis-joondalup.com.au/Unlock-the-Miracle-Within

Define Your Values

Johnhain [2]

Your values are the principles and beliefs that guide your decisions, actions, and priorities. Defining your values is crucial when you set out to clarify what matters most to you. Here's a step-by-step guide to help you define your values.

GUIDE TO DEFINING YOUR VALUES

1. **Self-Reflection:** Start by setting aside some dedicated time for self-reflection. Find a comfortable space to think deeply about your life and beliefs.
2. **Brainstorm:** Begin by brainstorming a list of words or phrases that resonate with you when you think about what's essential in life. These could be general concepts like *honesty*, *family*, *creativity*, *freedom*, and *adventure* or specific values related to your personal or professional life. Those values can be used in various contexts, such as personal development, decision-making, leadership, and so on. Feel free to choose any from this list that resonates with you or is relevant to your situation. Top of Form.
3. **Review Life Experiences:** Reflect on your past experiences, both positive and negative. Consider moments when you felt most fulfilled, proud, or content. What values were present in those moments? What were you doing or experiencing that made you feel that way?
4. **Identify Role Models:** Think about people you admire and respect. What qualities or values

do they possess that you find inspiring? These qualities may provide insights into your values.

5. **Prioritise Your List:** Review the values you have brainstormed and prioritise them. Try to narrow down the list to the most essential values that truly resonate with you. Consider which values are non-negotiable for you and which ones are less important.

6. **Define Each Value:** Take a moment to define each value on your list. Please write a brief description or statement for each value, to clarify what it means to you. For example, if one of your values is *family*, you might define it as *spending quality time with loved ones and prioritising their well-being*.

7. **Test Your Values:** Put your values to the test by applying them to real-life situations and decisions. Ask yourself if your choices align with your values. If your actions are inconsistent with your values, it may be a sign that you need to reassess and make adjustments.

8. **Create a Values Statement:** Develop a concise statement encapsulating your core values. This statement can serve as a personal mantra or a guiding principle for your life. For example,

"My core values are authenticity, compassion, and continuous learning".

9. **Share and Discuss:** Consider sharing your values with trusted friends, family members, or a therapist. Discussing your values with others can provide valuable insights and help reinforce your commitment to them.
10. **Revisit and Revise:** Your values may evolve as you grow and gain new experiences. Periodically revisit and revise your values to ensure they continue to reflect your beliefs and priorities.

Your values are a compass guiding you in significant life choices and everyday actions. Defining your values is a personal and ongoing process. It can help you make decisions that align with your authentic self and lead to a more meaningful and fulfilling life.

Life Balance

The more you are in balance within yourself and in your life, the better decisions you will make. Now that you have identified your values, you can set your priorities. We all have 24 hours a day. How do you want to spend your time? What is important to you? [17]

UNLOCK THE MIRACLE WITHIN

dimitrisvetsikas1969 [2]

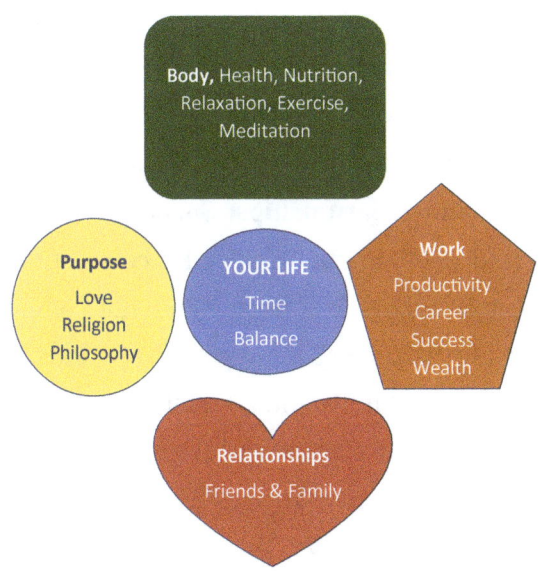

Life balance is the concept that guides you to find a harmonious equilibrium between the various aspects of life – work, family, personal interests, social activities, and self-care. A healthy life balance is essential for overall well-being and can lead to increased happiness, reduced stress, and improved physical and mental health.

The idea is to find the right balance for you. If relationships are important to you, you will not want to work 70 hours/week. Unfortunately, this is a concept not many people are aware of until they have lost their family, their health, or their purpose.

Here are some critical aspects of life balance:

Work: Having a fulfilling and rewarding career is essential, but overworking or excessive work-related stress can negatively impact other areas of your life. Setting boundaries, managing time effectively, and taking breaks can help you to maintain a healthy balance.

Family and Relationships: Spending quality time with loved ones, maintaining solid connections, and nurturing healthy relationships are vital components of your life balance. Balancing your work commitments with your family and social life is crucial.

Health and Self-Care: Prioritising your physical and mental well-being is essential. This includes regular exercise, a balanced diet, getting enough sleep, and taking time for relaxation and self-care activities like meditation or hobbies.

Personal Growth: Continuously learning and growing as an individual can contribute to a fulfilling life. Pursuing hobbies, setting personal goals, and engaging in self-improvement activities can help you find balance.

Time Management: Effective time management skills are critical for balancing various responsibilities. This involves setting priorities, creating schedules, and avoiding procrastination.

Boundaries: Establishing clear boundaries between work and personal life is crucial. This means not letting work spill over into your time and vice versa.

Flexibility: Recognise that life is dynamic, and there may be times when certain aspects require more attention than others. Being adaptable and adjusting your priorities as needed is vital to maintaining balance.

Stress Management: Developing healthy coping mechanisms for stress, such as mindfulness, relaxation techniques, hypnotherapy or seeking support from a therapist, can help you manage the challenges that life throws your way.

Reflection and Evaluation: Regularly assess your life balance to see if any areas need adjustment. This can help you stay on track and make necessary changes when your circumstances or priorities shift.

Setting Realistic Expectations: Be realistic about what you can accomplish in a given day or week. Setting overly ambitious goals can lead to burnout and imbalance.

Life balance is a personal and ever-evolving concept. What works for one person may not work for another. Finding the balance that aligns with your values, goals, and circumstances is essential. Regular self-reflection and adjustment are crucial to maintaining a fulfilling and balanced life.

The 80/20 Rule

The 80/20 rule (also known as the Pareto principle) is a crucial strategy for effective time management. The aim is to invest 20% of your energy to get an 80% result. For example, you might spend two hours on a specific task, and the result is good but imperfect. Now, the question is, would spending another eight hours in the same way be worthwhile to make it 20% better?

Decide what is essential for you, and link that with your values. Then, schedule your time for what is most important to you, and use the 80/20 principle for efficient time management.

Read through the detailed explanation below and think carefully about your life. Where would 20% of effort be sufficient in your time segment, and where is it essential to spend 100% energy and time?

Then, apply this principle to the previous segment on life balance.

Here is the theory of the Pareto Principle:

Also called the law of the vital few, it is a concept that suggests that roughly 80% of outcomes or effects result from 20% of causes or inputs. This principle was named after Italian economist Vilfredo Pareto, who observed in the early 20th century that 80% of the land in Italy was owned by 20% of the population.

The 80/20 rule has since been applied to various fields and contexts, including business, economics, and time management, to highlight the idea that smaller portions of effort or resources often produce the majority of results or benefits. Some common examples of the 80/20 rule include:

Business Sales: In business, it's often observed that 20% of customers contribute to 80% of revenue or profits. This insight can help companies focus their marketing and customer service efforts on their most valuable customers.

Time Management: People may find that 20% of their tasks or activities are responsible for 80% of their productivity or satisfaction. Individuals can use their time more effectively by identifying and prioritising these high-impact tasks.

Product Quality: In manufacturing or software development, it's common to discover that 20% of defects or issues cause 80% of customer complaints. Addressing these critical issues can lead to significant improvements in product quality.

Personal Finance: Some individuals might notice that they spend 20% of their income on expenses that account for 80% of their financial stress. They can achieve better financial stability by reducing or managing these significant expenses.

It's important to note that the 80/20 split is a general guideline rather than a strict rule. Sometimes the ratio might be different, such as 70/30 or 90/10. Still, the principle remains the same: a minority of factors often disproportionately and significantly impact the overall outcome. The 80/20 rule can be a valuable tool for prioritisation and resource allocation in various aspects of life and business.

Goal Setting

At last, how to set your goals. This chapter is like a summary of all 5 Steps and guides you through a comprehensive process. The hypnosis session for goal setting and navigation will support you in this process and in achieving your goals.

Here is where to find the Hypnosis Session:
https://hypnosis-joondalup.com.au/miracle-login

**Step 5 Live Your Life on Your Terms –
Hypnosis for future vision and goal setting.**

GOAL SETTING

ArtsyBee [2]

Setting your goals in life is a necessary process that can provide you with direction, motivation, and a sense of purpose. Here's a step-by-step guide to help you set meaningful life goals.

SETTING MEANINGFUL LIFE GOALS

Self-Reflection: Reflect on your values, passions, and what truly matters to you. Consider your strengths, weaknesses, and the things that make you happy. Ask yourself questions like:

What are my core values and beliefs?
What do I enjoy doing in my free time?
What are my talents and strengths?
What kind of lifestyle do I want to lead?

Define the Different Areas of Your Life: Divide your life into different areas or categories, such as career, relationships, health, personal development, finances, and leisure. This will enable you to identify clear goals in those aspects of your life.

SMART Goals: Use the SMART criteria to create specific, measurable, achievable, relevant, and time-bound goals. SMART goals are more concrete and actionable, making it easier to track your progress. For example:

Specific: Clearly define what you want to achieve.

Measurable: Determine how you will measure your progress.

Achievable: Ensure the goal is realistic and attainable.

Relevant: Align the goal with your values and priorities.

Time-bound: Set a deadline for achieving the goal.

Short-Term and Long-Term Goals: Distinguish between short-term goals (achievable within the next few months to a year) and long-term goals (those you want to achieve in the next 5, 10, or 20 years). Short-term goals can help you make progress toward your long-term goals.

Prioritise Goals: Not all goals are equally important or urgent. Prioritise your goals according to their significance and impact on your life. This will help you focus your time and energy on what matters most.

Break Goals Down: Divide larger, more complex goals into smaller, manageable steps. This makes it easier to take consistent action and maintain motivation.

Create an Action Plan: Develop a detailed action plan for each goal. Specify what you need to do, when, and how. Include milestones to measure your progress along the way.

Stay Accountable: Share your goals with a trusted friend, family member, or mentor who can hold you accountable and provide support and encouragement.

Regularly Review and Adjust: Periodically review your goals and assess your progress. Adjust them in line with changing circumstances, experiences, or personal growth.

Stay Motivated: Keep your motivation high by visualising your success, celebrating small achievements, and reminding yourself why your goals are important to you.

Seek Feedback: Don't hesitate to seek feedback from others who have experience in the areas you're pursuing. Their insights can be invaluable in guiding your efforts.

Practise Patience: It often takes time and perseverance to achieve meaningful life goals. Be patient and stay committed to your journey.

Remember that setting life goals is a dynamic process. As you grow and evolve, your goals may also change. Stay flexible and adapt your goals to align with your evolving values and aspirations.

Please share your journey and ask some questions to the related Facebook group:
https://hypnosis-joondalup.com.au/Unlock-the-Miracle-Within

CHECKLIST

Defining Your Values
Notes:
_____
_____
_____

Life Balance
Notes:
_____
_____
_____

The 80/ 20 rule – crucial for time management
Notes:
_____
_____
_____

Goal Setting
Notes:
_____
_____
_____

FINAL THOUGHTS

Just for a moment, imagine that you, your family, your friends, and the people around you are all living with the knowledge that they are as God created them. Each person profoundly believes that they are unique, loved, and beautiful. How would your world look and feel? There would be no comparison, no competing against each other. Everybody would know they are uniquely created and here to fulfil their destiny.

I wrote this book with this vision in my mind. I was visualising people getting along with each other, living with love and compassion, supporting each other, uplifting each other with compliments, and being grateful for themselves and others.

What if we all continuously sought to live with more compassion and kindness, keep learning and improving, and create more beauty and love.

What if we could seek uplifting ways to communicate to ourselves and others? What if we explored new ways of thinking and creating a world that syncs with all creation?

Writing this book has been an uplifting and gratifying process for me. I hope it has been as inspirational and life-improving for you as it has been for me. As you share this book with others, more lives will be changed, and my vision for my world will come closer to fulfilment, so I thank you.

Thank you from the depths of my heart for starting this process in your unique environment. I am looking forward to reading about your life transformation on the Facebook group, or drop me an email at ursula@hypnosis-joondalup.com.au.

To an inspirational life

Ursula Knecht

Clinical Hypnotherapist
0468 858 466
ursula@hypnosis-joondalup.com.au
https://hypnosis-joondalup.com.au

REFERENCES

1. Institute T linguist. Napoleon Hill. THINK AND GROW RICH, Chapter 2 (1) [Internet]. lingq.com. [cited 2023 Sep 5] Available from: https://www.lingq.com/en/learn-english-online/courses/158842/chapter-2-1-414171/

2. 4.1 million+ Stunning Free Images to Use Anywhere - Pixabay - Pixabay [Internet]. [cited 2023 Sep 6]. Available from: https://pixabay.com/

3. Berg IK. The Miracle Question [Internet] [cited 2023 Sep 5]. Available from: https://www.psychotherapy.net/interview/insoo-kim-berg#section-solution-focused-model

4. Knecht UD. Back Pain Goodbye, Overcome Back Pain & Reclaim Your Life in 12 weeks or less; 2019.

5. Emoto M. Masaru Emoto's Experiment in GratitudeNo Title [Internet]. [cited 2023 Sep 5]. Available from: https://youtu.be/SDNhH8deZPg?si=CPt3Bhg8pBENq84j

6. EMOTO M. SCIENCE OF WATER [Internet]. [cited 2023 Sep 5]. Available from: https://masaru-emoto.net/en/crystal-2/

7. Foundation For Inner Peace. A Course In Miracle. Workbook f. Nebrska: Course in Miracle Society; 2016.

8. Genesis 1 [Internet] [cited 2023 Sep 5]. Available from: https://biblehub.com/niv/genesis/1.htm

9. Chi C. LEVELS OF VIBRATION (a beginner's guide) [Internet]. 2022. Available from: https://en.rattibha.com/thread/1508576946199932933

10. Life's Energy Chart by Sir David R. Hawkins, M.D., Ph.D. [Internet]. [cited 2023 Sep 5]. Available from: https://www.taoaruba.org/lifes-energy-chart

11. Coffee B. RAISING VIBRATIONS [Internet]. BLUESTONES COFFEE; 2022. Available from: https://bluestonescoffee.co.uk/raising-vibrations

12. Kropotov JD. Beta Wave. [Internet]. [cited 2023 Sep 5]. Available from: https://www.sciencedirect.com/topics/medicine-and-dentistry/beta-wave

13. Nummenmaa L, Glerean E, Hari R, Hietanen JK. Bodily maps of emotions. Proceedings of the National Academy of Sciences. 2013 Dec 30;111(2):646–51. Available from: https://www.pnas.org/doi/10.1073/pnas.1321664111

14. Gloom, 5 Types Of Brain Waves Frequencies: Gamma, Beta, Alpha, Theta, Delta [Internet]. Mental Health Daily. 2014. Available from: https://mentalhealthdaily.com/2014/04/15/5-types-of-brain-waves-frequencies-gamma-beta-alpha-theta-delta/

15. Comfort in God's Presence: A Psalm 23:4 Devotional — Bible Lyfe [Internet]. [cited 2023 Sep 5]. Available from: https://www.biblelyfe.com/verse-of-the-day/meaning-of-psalm-23-4

16. The Greatest Inventor "Thomas Alva Edison's" vision on Failures. [Internet]. [cited 2023 Sep 5]. Available from: https://www.linkedin.com/pulse/greatest-inventor-thomas-alva-edisons-vision-failures-narayanan

17. J.Seiwert L. 30 Minuten fuer Zeit -Balance. Offenbach; 2001.

www.ingramcontent.com/pod-product-compliance
Lightning Source LLC
LaVergne TN
LVHW020138080526
838202LV00048B/3969